Nutcrackers
AND
PIRATES

A Boy's Journey Into Dance

by Charmain Zimmerman Brackett

Illustration and Design by Ashlee Henry

ISBN: 978-0-9856259-9-3

The book is dedicated to all the male dancers out there who followed their passions and dreams for being on stage instead of letting people talk them out of it.

Special thanks to Jessica Brackett Carroll, Marian Lambert-Yu and Rachel Bishop.

Sports are important to a lot of people. My dad played soccer when he was growing up. He even played it in college. When I was younger, I played soccer and baseball. I liked sports, but I wasn't the fastest on the team. I started to think sports weren't my thing, but what else could I do?

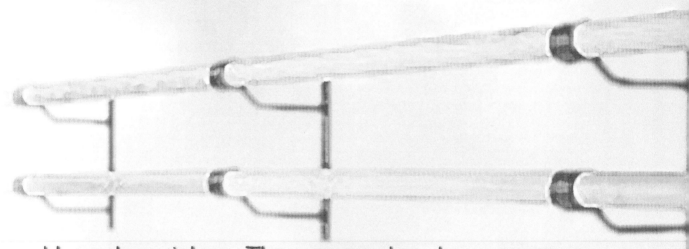

I have two sisters. They never played soccer or baseball. They liked to dance. They danced on stage and wore costumes. Some people might think dance is just for girls, but it's more than that. Dance is for everyone. Boys can dance too.

At Christmas, my sisters were in a ballet called the Nutcracker. I was 6 when I saw my first Nutcracker ballet. It is about a little girl named Clara whose uncle gives her a toy nutcracker at a Christmas party. It's ugly, but she likes it. Her brother breaks it, and it makes her sad. But her uncle fixes it. Later that night after everyone has gone to sleep, she sneaks out to the tree where she left it. All of a sudden, the Christmas tree begins to grow. Big, scary mice surround Clara. Then she sees her nutcracker is taller than she is. He's alive and leading a group of toy soldiers to save them all from the mice. He saves Clara, but the mouse king hurts him. When Clara goes to help the nutcracker, she finds that he's been turned into a prince.

It starts to snow. They travel through the snow to a place called the Land of the Sweets, where she meets all kinds of dancers including the Sugar Plum Fairy and her Cavalier. They dance together. He picks her up a lot, and at the end, the Cavalier holds her above his head as he walks around the stage to the music. When I saw this for the first time, I turned to my mother.

"He's strong. I want to do that," I told her.

She smiled and nodded.

A few weeks later, my mother enrolled me in ballet classes at the same studio where my sisters danced.

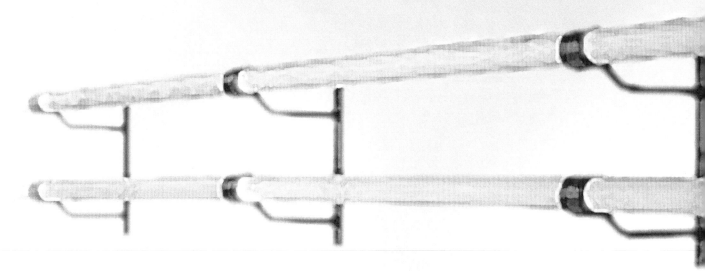

There weren't a lot of boys taking classes, mainly girls. I wasn't sure why because dance is a type of exercise except to music. The girls wore leotards to class, but boys wore a white t-shirt and a black pair of shorts. I thought it was fun to take ballet.

The next year I danced in my first Nutcracker. I was a soldier and got to fight the mice who attacked Clara. We got to dance with wooden swords.,

I've danced in a lot of different shows. I've been a fierce wolf, a one-handed pirate who danced with a sword, and a kingly lion who saved the world from an evil ice queen.

I also learned more about dance in other countries. People dance for many reasons, and the biggest one is to celebrate. It's not just women who dance. Men dance too.

One of the dances in the Nutcracker is sometimes called Russian. It's one of my favorites. It's often based on the Cossack dance from the Ukraine. They danced it more than 500 years ago after men returned from battle.

Some of the movements include kicks and jumps. My favorite is the toe touch when a man jumps in the air and touches the tips of his toes with his fingers. They are hard to do.

In the United States, dance is an important part of Native American culture, and for hundreds of years, men have danced to tell stories or to celebrate. The costumes they wear depend on their different tribes, but many of them use bird feathers, beads, and bells on their clothes. Sometimes they dance with props such as hoops, and when they do war dances, they dance with spears and shields. They also have sacred dances. Native Americans continue to keep their traditions alive and hold competitions at Pow Wows.

Men in Africa dance for the same reasons. There are more than 800 ethnic groups in Africa; each has a different type of dance. They use dance to mark important times in people's lives and celebrate their births and deaths.

One group called the Massai has a jumping dance to show a boy is becoming a man. They perform this dance during a 10-day ceremony. They try to jump as high as they can while keeping their entire body straight. It proves their strength and stamina as warriors.

Besides taking ballet at the studio, I take modern dance at school. They also teach tap, jazz, and African dance.

At my school, we even have a class just for the guys. Sometimes we throw some break dance moves into the pieces we work on. That's fun. I like break dance a lot.

I found I could dance other places besides the ballet and school. I've danced in musicals with some of the local community theater groups and the college.

The more I danced the more I remembered my original reason to dance. I wanted to be able to do those lifts I saw when I was little. So I started working out with weights and working on my strength. And I began taking partnering classes to learn the proper way to lift a ballerina and walk with her high above my head without anyone getting hurt. And one year, it happened. I was cast as the Cavalier in The Nutcracker, and I did get to lift the Sugar Plum Fairy high over my head and walk around the stage with her. My mom was proud and cried happy tears that day.

Jeremy Brackett started dancing at the age of 6. He's danced in numerous productions of the Nutcracker and branched out into community musical theater dancing in multiple roles with different theater companies. He dances because he enjoys it, and yes, dancers are strong.